Risk
Management
Explained

Can Akdeniz

First Publishing, 2015

ISBN-10: 978-1507681855
ISBN-13: 1507681852

Baderstrasse 55
D-53489 Bad Bodendorf
Germany

Web: http://www.bestbusinessbooks.co

Contents

Introduction

If you could choose one superpower, just one, what would it be? Would you like to fly, or see through walls and clothing? Would you like to read other people's minds, and freak them out by answering questions they were yet to ask? Would you perhaps like the power to shape shift, or even move through solid objects like walls?

While all these powers are great, and having just one of them might greatly change your life, one superpower stands head and shoulders above the rest: ***The ability to predict the future!*** Imagine if you could see what was going to happen in the immediate and not so immediate future, with remarkable accuracy, and thereby avoid getting caught up in the wrong place at the wrong time? What a wonderful life it would be!

Unfortunately, we do not live in that world. You've heard it said before that the best way to predict the future is to plan for it, and this is very true. One of the best ways to plan for the future is to manage the risks associated with the future you are planning, and mitigating or eliminating these risks altogether. Fortunately, ***risk management*** is a superpower that you can develop with practice. It is a skill that you can learn over time!

The following short chapters will run you through the ambit of just what risk management is. They will show you how you can apply it to your business. We will discuss the principles of risk management, and the processes involved, and also give you an idea of the application of these processes to a couple of businesses.

The rules of risk management are mostly universal, and by tweaking them slightly, you can apply them to any enterprise. You will be armed with the essential tools to devise a risk management strategy that will, in effect, maximize the potential of your business to realize opportunities. This is, after all, the ultimate purpose of risk management!

Risk is, in short, *the effect that uncertainty and unplanned event will have on your objectives.* It is based on the possibility that these events might occur, and the impact that these will have on you organizations ability to meet its goals. Risk takes on many forms, depending on the nature of your company, and these include *IT and network security risks, operational and personnel risks, and financial risks.*

Identifying, assessing, and prioritizing these risks through coordinated, economical applications of available resources in order to minimize, monitor and control the impact of these risks on your business is the short definition of risk management. You can also minimize the probability of these unfortunate events, with the application of a solid risk management strategy.

Projects fail all the time, and they do so at various stages in their design, development or production. Credit risk, legal liabilities, accidents and natural disasters all take their toll on your business. Understanding risk management can help you successfully manage these threats, and really make a success out of your enterprise!

The Principles Of Risk Management

Various bodies around the world have identified a number of principles of risk management, and it is accepted that risk management should meet at least some of these criteria. It is important to note that you should set out on your strategy with very specific objectives in mind, and as a result, managing risk for your business should incorporate the following, at least:

- It is essential that it *creates value*. The resources you use to mitigate the risk should be considerably less than the consequences of going nothing.
- You should include risk management as an integral part of your organizational processes.
- It should be included in all your business decisions.
- Uncertainties and assumptions should be addressed explicitly.
- The process of risk management should be structured and systematic.
- You should base your strategy on the highest quality of information that is available.
- It should be flexible and easily tailored to meet your changing circumstances.
- Human factors should be taken into account.
- Transparency and inclusivity are imperative.
- You need to design you strategy in a way that is dynamic and highly responsive to change.
- It should be able to improve and be continually enhanced.
- Re-assessment is critical and your strategy for risk management should be continually or periodically re-assessed.

The methods of application for risk management will depend largely on context in which they are applied. These contexts vary greatly, from project management, public health and safety, financial portfolios, industrial processes, engineering, through to security and actuarial assessments. As far as strategy goes, you can either transfer this threat to a third party, avoid the threat, reduce the impact, or accept the potential consequences of this threat.

Ideally, your approach to risk management should be such that you mitigate the greatest threats first, handling those risks that have a lower probability of actually happening after this, in descending order. Often, you will find that in practice you find it difficult to balance resources used to mitigate higher risks with lower loss, with those that have a high loss but lower probability of occurring.

Risk falls into a number of categories. Your business might be faced with just one of these risks, or all of them, but understanding them will get you some ways in developing your strategy for mitigation:

Intangible risk management is that risk with 100% probability of happening, but which your company ignores because you were unable to identify it in the first place.

Relationship risk results from ineffective collaboration.

Process-engagement risk is where ineffective procedures are applied on an operational level.

Now, these risks may reduce productivity, decrease cost-effectiveness, service, quality, reputation, brand value, earnings quality, and ultimately profitability. While resources spent on risk management could have been put to better use to increase profit, ideal risk management minimizes not only the manpower and resources used, but also the negative effects.

1. The Method And The Process Of Risk Management

Depending on the level of sophistication of your business, how you apply the risk management principles above could vary considerably. However, let us simplify this process for you. You can follow method to your strategy, and you will very quickly come to grips with the order of approach that you need to take, especially if you are to enjoy continued success in your business.

The first step is to identify the threats or possible threats. Characterizing these threats will give you immediate insight as to how you should go about developing your strategy. You then need to assess your critical assets' vulnerability to these threats. Thirdly, you need to determine the expected likelihood/consequence of these threats on your assets. Following which, you need to determine ways in which you can reduce these risks. Finally, based on a solid strategy, you need to prioritize risk reduction measures.

Now that you understand the method to the madness, let us go through the process of risk management. It consists of a number of steps, and once you get your head around these, you will really be well on your way.

Establish Context

Context is incredibly important, in every aspect of your life. You operate in contexts all the time, and establishing context when it comes to risk management is critical. Before you ask how to do this, don't worry. Here is how:

- Identify the risk in your specific area of operation
- Plan thoroughly the remainder of the process
- Map out the social scope of risk management and the identity and objectives of all stakeholders
- Map out the constraints associated, and the basis upon which you will evaluate the risks
- Define a framework for the activity
- Define an agenda for identification
- Develop an analysis of the risks involved in the process
- Develop or mitigate solutions to the risks using available resources, be they technological, human or organizational

Identification

Once you establish the context, you need to set about identifying all the potential risks. Risks can cause problems, or be beneficial (as in, problems experienced by your competitors) to your enterprise, and you need to know what these events are before they are triggered. You can start by identifying the source of your problems, or you can start with the problem itself.

Analysing the source of the risk or problem is one approach. The sources of these risks could be internal or external to your business, and these risks need to be mitigated. Risks usually involve factors that cannot be managed, so you should focus on mitigating these risks, instead of on managing them. The weather over the ocean or airport, the stakeholders of a project, or even the employees of your company are all examples of risk sources.

Analysing the actual problem is slightly different. Here you are dealing with identified threats. The threats to confidential information or the threat of human error are just some of these. The threat could come from a number of entities, shareholders, customers, or legislative authorities like the government, to name but a few.

When you know the source or the problem, you can then investigate the events that could result because of this source, or the events that may lead to a problem. Your chosen method of identification will depend on your company culture, or on industry practice and compliance. Below are a couple of methods for identifying risks that are common today.

- *Common-risk checking*: There are lists with known risks that are available in several industries, and you can check these lists to see if they apply to you and your business.

- *Scenario-based risk identification*: In this type of identification, you create different scenarios, which may be alternatives to achieving your business objectives, or simply an analysis of how forces interact in a market. The events that trigger undesired scenario alternatives are then listed as risks.

- *Risk charting*: This is a combination of all the listed approaches to identification, and lists the resources at risk, threats, and modifying factors as well as consequences to avoid.

- *Objective-based risk identification*: Anything that may put you at risk of not achieving your company's objective is identified as a risk.

- *Taxonomy-based risk identification:* This is a breakdown of possible risk sources, and based on this taxonomy, a questionnaire is compiled the answers to which will reveal risks.

Assessment

Now that you have identified the risks, an assessment must be made of the potential to do harm. Added to the severity of impact, you need to assess the probability of occurrence. These values could be simple, as in the cost of losing a building, or immeasurable, as the case of an unlikely event possibly occurring. The assessment process is therefore critical when it comes to making the most educated decisions in order to prioritize properly the implementation of your risk management plan.

2. The Composite Risk Index

Let us now get a little bit technical. There is no need to worry, this is just one formula that you need to know if you are to get the basics right.

The Composite Risk Index is as follows:

Composite Risk Index = Impact Of Risk Event x Probability Of Occurrence

That's it. Really!

The scale by which risk impact is measured is usually 1-5. The number 1 represents the minimum impact of the risk occurrence, and 5 is the maximum possible impact. The probability of occurrence is also assessed on the same scale, where 1 is low probability, and 5 is very high probability of occurrence. This could be expressed in mathematical terms, i.e. the event occurs once in ten years, or once in 100 years, or it may be expressed in words, i.e. the event occurs very often, or the event has been known to occur!

The Composite Risk Index can thus take values from about 1-25. This range is divided usually into three sub-ranges. Overall risk assessment is therefore typically Low, Medium or High, but this depends on the sub-range that contains the calculated value of the Composite Risk Index!

You must be aware though, that the probability that an event will occur is difficult to estimate. This is because past data of the frequency of these occurrences is not always readily available, and probability is definitely not certainty. The impact of risk is also difficult to estimate, since the potential loss is difficult to estimate in the event of certain risk factors occurring.

Changes in the business environment can also result in these factors changing in magnitude. Risk avoidance and prevention measures also come into play here. You therefore need to re-assess these risks periodically, and make the necessary adjustments to your mitigation measures as these become necessary.

3. Risk Options

You will usually formulate risk mitigation measures according to one of these risk options:

- The design of a totally new business process, with built-in risk control measures to begin with.

- Periodical re-assessment of the accepted risks as a part of your business's operations, modifying mitigation measures as you go

- Transferring risks to external agencies such as insurance companies

- Or complete avoidance of risks altogether

You will find that the benefits of risk management depend largely on how your risk assessment is performed.

You must be able to present your risk assessment findings in market, financial and schedule terms, especially in business today.

Potential Risk Treatments

How you handle the risks after you have identified and assessed them is the next step. Managing risk usually falls into one of these categories:

- Avoidance
- Reduction
- Sharing
- Retention

Risk Avoidance

This involves not doing anything that has even the possibility of risk, for example, not driving a car in case you get hijacked or have an accident, not going to the mall in case you get mugged, or not buying a building because you do not want to assume any of the legal liability that goes with it.

While avoidance removes all the risks from your life and business, it also means that you miss potential profits that accepting certain risks might have allowed. Avoiding getting into business to cut out the potential for loss also cuts you off from possible profits. Increasing risk regulation in hospitals, for example, has seen them avoid treating high-risk conditions, taking on patients that present a lower risk.

This is not good for patients who present a higher risk, and it is the same in business. Avoiding risks could see you living life on the side-lines, and this is definitely nowhere to make any real money.

Hazard Prevention

This is the prevention of risks in an emergency. The most effective part of hazard prevention is the first part, which involves eliminating the hazard. This stage is followed by mitigation if it takes too long or is too costly, however.

Risk Reduction

Risk reduction is also known as optimization. It involves reducing the likelihood of loss. An example is a fire extinguisher, designed to put out fires, to reduce the risk of loss by fire. However, you might cause damage with the foam from the extinguisher, so you would need to mitigate these two risks. Perhaps a fire suppression system could be more suitable to your needs.

You need to acknowledge that risks can be positive, or negative. You will therefore need to find a balance between negative risk and the benefit of the activity. You also need to find a balance between risk reduction and effort applied. Your aim is to achieve levels of risk that you can tolerate.

Risk Sharing

When you share the burden of loss from a risk with another party in an effort to reduce the risk, this is known as risk sharing. However, the term 'risk transfer' is also used, mistakenly believing that you can transfer a risk to someone else, through insurance or outsourcing. Realistically though, if the insurance company goes bankrupt, then the risk goes back to the first party. Therefore, we will just keep it simple, and use the term **risk sharing**.

Risk Retention

This is an acceptance of the loss from risk, when it occurs. This is viable for smaller risks, when the total cost of insuring would be greater than the total loss sustained over time. Risks that are transferred, or ones that are not avoided, are retained, by default. Included in this are risks that are so large or catastrophic that they cannot be insured or their premiums will be unfeasible.

Can Akdeniz

4. Creating A Risk Management Plan

The risk management plan should put forward effective controls for managing risks. A high risk of computer viruses, for example, could be mitigated by the implementation of antivirus software. Good risk management plans contain a schedule for control implementation, as well as the people responsible for the actions. You should select appropriate controls that will measure each risk, and the risk mitigation should be approved by the level of management that is appropriate to the risk!

After you have completed the risk assessment phase, you need to prepare a Risk Treatment Plan. This should document the decisions on how to handle each of the risks identified. Selecting security controls is a part of risk mitigation, one which should be stated in a Statement of Applicability. This statement identifies the particular controls that have been selected from the standard and why!

Implementation

This is the logical next step after planning. You've heard the saying, proper planning prevents poor performance, and it is no different when it comes to mitigating the effects of risks. The implementation phase should contain each of the applicable measures listed above. You can *transfer* risk to an insurer by purchasing insurance policies for those risks that you have decided need to be transferred.

Avoiding the risks that can safely be avoided is also a part of implementation, a necessary part, even though avoiding risks very seldom has any real benefit, other than sticking your head in the sand. You need to therefore only avoid those risks that do not satisfy any of your goals. *Reduce* and *retain* the remainder of your risks. DO not force all of these strategies into your risk implementation plan, however, if they are not applicable.

Review And Evaluation Of The Plan

Like most things in life, you will not get your risk management plan completely right the first time. In fact, by its very nature, a risk management plan is an evolving document that lends itself to changes from time to time. With practice, you will get it close to perfect for sure, but it will never be absolutely perfect. Experience and actual losses will make it necessary to change the plan often. As you feed information into your plan, different decisions will be possible when you deal with the risks at hand.

Needless to say, you should update your risk analysis results periodically. This will lead to periodic updates of your risk management plan as well. There are many reasons why this is essential. Of primary concern, is whether the controls that you have in place are still applicable. Another reason for these periodic updates is whether or not these selected security controls are still effective. Your business is constantly changing, as are the risks that you are exposed to, so you need to evaluate these possible risk level changes.

Limitation

You need to be careful though, that you do not hold yourself back with excessive risk management. Making risk management a priority, excessively, could be a serious hindrance when it comes to completing projects. You might become so paralyzed by the potential risk that you do not even get started. It is therefore detrimental to your business if you are of the view that other activities should be halted until you are comfortable that your risk management process is complete. Remember that there is a clear distinction between *uncertainty* and *risk*!

Remember too, that you could waste a lot of time dealing with unlikely risks if you assess and prioritize these risks incorrectly. You might divert resources that could be utilized more profitably by spending too much time managing risks that are unlikely to occur. While we know that these unlikely events are possible, you should remember that sometimes it is better to retain this risk, and simply deal with the consequences if the loss does occur.

Qualitative risk assessment is subjective at best, and it lacks consistency. Formal risk assessment is therefore best justified by legal or bureaucratic processes!

Can Akdeniz

5. Possible Areas Of Risk Management

Think for a minute about **corporate finance**. In this context, risk management is the technique used to measure, monitor, and control the operational and financial risk to your business' balance sheet. You can use the Basel II framework to break down risks into market risk, credit risk, and operational risk. This framework also specifies calculation methods as these relate to capital requirements for every one of these components!

Let us now go through a few other **possible areas of risk management**.

Enterprise Risk Management

As far as businesses and companies go, **enterprise risk management** is probably the most applicable. This is where an event or circumstance that could possibly occur might have negative influences on your business. This is important, because the very existence of your enterprise could be impacted. Human resources and capital, products and services, customers, markets, and even the environment in which your business operates could also be impacted. As with the previous example of a financial institution, enterprise risk management constitutes of a number of elements:

- Credit Risk
- Interest Rate Risk
- Asset Liability Management
- Liquidity Risk
- Market Risk
- Operational Risk

In general, however, every possible risk should have a pre-formulated plan that is set to handle possible consequences, setting in place contingencies, should the risk become a liability.

Let us get technical for a minute again, and give you some crucial information on possible estimates that your project manager can make, from the **average cost/employer over time**, also known as the **cost accrual ratio**:

- You can estimate the costs associated with particular risks if they arise by multiplying the employer costs per time unit by an estimation of the time lost
- You can estimate the probable increase in time as this pertains to the risk, usually called the schedule variance due to risk. This puts the highest risks to the schedule first, so that the greatest risks are minimized as quickly as possible. Note however, that this can be a little misleading
- Another estimate that can be made is the probable increase in cost associated with the particular risk, also known as **the cost variance due to risk**. This puts the highest risk to the overall budget first, and allows you to see concerns about schedule variance since this is an actual function of it

Risks to your project or process can come from two very specific sources. They can be due to *Special Cause Variation*, or they can be caused as a result of *Common Cause Variation*. Both of these require appropriate treatments, and you should therefore be aware of the source of the risk. Special causes and common causes are pretty self-explanatory, and you should just make the necessary adjustments to your risk management plan as applicable.

Medical Device Risk Management

If you are in the business of creating and developing medical devices, you need to identify, evaluate and mitigate the risks associated with damage to the environment or property, or harm that could be caused to people. This is the approach of your risk management strategy. Risk management is very important for these reasons when it comes to the design and development of medical devices. It is applicable to any type of medical device, and pertains also to the processes involved in their production, as well as their field experience evaluation.

It is a prerequisite of almost every regulatory body, including the FDA, and is in fact considered a safety standard. This provides you with the framework for the processes, as well as the associated requirements for management responsibilities. Included in this framework are also the analysis of risks and their evaluation, controls, and the lifecycle risk management.

There are a number of techniques that are typical to the medical device industry, and these include the following:

- Hazard Analysis
- Fault Free Analysis
- Failure Mode and Effect Analysis
- The Hazard and Operability Study, and
- Risk Traceability Analysis

Some of these require diagramming software, while others are easily accomplished on simple spreadsheet programs. Integrated risk management solutions for medical devices are also available.

Project Management and its Risk Management Applications

Most businesses engage in projects from time to time. Sometimes your core business is project management, and if this is the case, then the following activities should be included in your risk management strategy:

- Risk management is very specific to each individual project. You need to plan how you will manage each risk for each particular project, with the specifics of the project in mind. Your plan should include tasks associated with management and responsibilities, budget and activities.
- You risk officer should not be the same member of your team as your project manager. The risk officer should be exclusively responsible for the foresight of any potential problems with the project. While your risk officer should be optimistic about the overall success of the project, they should also display a healthy measure of scepticism.
- You should maintain a live project risk database. With each risk, you should have an opening date, title, a short description, the risk's probability, and its importance. You can also assign a person who will handle the risk by a specific date.
- You can also create an anonymous risk-reporting avenue, one where each member has the possibility of reporting risk that they foresee with the project.
- Once you have chosen which of the project risks are to be mitigated, you should prepare the mitigation plans for these risks. In your mitigation plan, you need

to describe how you plan to handle these particular risks in order to avoid it altogether, or at least minimize the consequences if the risk becomes a reality.

- You should also develop a summary of planned and faced risks, as well as the effectiveness of the mitigation measures you executed, as well as the efforts spent in your risk management exercise.

Risk Management For Infrastructure

This applies particularly to construction companies, or ones involved in property development and management. These megaprojects are mostly large-scale investment projects, and could typically cost more than a billion dollars. However, smaller-scale project use mostly the same principles, as the risk management principles and processes applied are generally the same. Infrastructure projects include highways, tunnels, bridges, airports and railways. Dams, wastewater projects, public buildings and defence systems are also included in these types of projects. The risk to these projects comes from a number of sources, including safety, finance, social impacts and environmental impacts. Special methods are continually being developed for this type of risk management all the time!

Risk Management Regarding Natural Disasters

Natural disasters affect every business. Floods and earthquakes do not choose where they strike, or whom. They come quickly, and they destroy everything in their wake. It is therefore imperative that you make an assessment of the risks associated with natural disasters, especially if your area of operation is one that is prone to these events. Future repair costs, downtime, business interruption losses, effects on the environment, insurance, and the cost of reducing this risk are all results of this risk management that make it valuable.

Risk Management Regarding Information Technology

If your business is not affected or influenced by information technology then you are probably not doing something right. IT has invaded practically every sector of business today. Information technology risk is a very new term, born from a need for information security to be protected. Information security is just one part of many risks related to IT, as well as the real-world processes supported by this industry. Many methodologies have been created to handle this type of risk, and almost all of these methods are specific to their niche in the IT industry. You will do well to partner your enterprise risk management with your IT risk management, and marry the two effectively to foresee any possible risks or problems that could come out of the woodwork. This marriage will serve your risk management strategy rather effectively, and you will reap the rewards of the combined efforts of these two mostly related avenues of risk management.

Risk Management In The Petroleum and Natural Gas Industry

The safety case regime regulates the operational risk management for the offshore oil and gas industry. The international standard ISO 17776:2000 lists hazard identification and risk assessment tools, as well as techniques. Organisations like the International Association of Drilling Contractors have a published list of guidelines based on this standard. Safety case submissions by governments usually contain diagrammatic representations of hazardous events, as part of their risk management strategy. Mining, health, aviation, industrial, defence and finance are amongst the industries that use this technique.

Risk Management As Applied In Pharmaceutical Industries

Aspects including development, distribution, manufacturing, and inspection/submission and review processes are amongst the principles and tools used in the application of quality risk management in the pharmaceutical sector. This is applied to the lifecycles of drug substances, drug products, as well as biological and biotechnological products. These could also include the raw materials, solvents, packaging and labelling materials used in drug products, biological and biotechnological products. You can also apply risk management to the assessment of microbiological contamination, as this relates to pharmaceutical products as well as cleanroom manufacturing environments.

Can Akdeniz

6. Positive Risk Management Explained

People have vastly different appetites for risk. Some can handle it, and others, well, they just cannot. Positive Risk Management recognizes this, and the importance of the human factor. Drawing from the work of academics and professionals, it takes into account the human dimension of risk, emphasizing it in fact.

Firstly, Positive Risk Management recognizes that any situation can be rendered hazardous, simply because of the involvement of someone with little appetite risk. This can come from both extremes, whether the person is too much towards risk taking, or if they are too risk averse.

Secondly, it recognizes risk as an inevitable and present element part of life. This ranges from our conception right through to the end of our lives when we lose our battle with life-threatening risk.

Thirdly, it recognizes that every individual has a particular orientation towards risk; while at one extreme people may by nature be timid, anxious and fearful, others will be adventurous, impulsive and almost oblivious to danger. These differences are evident in the way we drive our cars, in our diets, in our relationships, in our careers.

Finally, Positive Risk Management recognizes that risk is an essential part of business. In fact, any activity in life comes with risks, as have all the initiatives that have contributed to our success and civilization. Even many enjoyable activities involve a willingness to take risks.

The lack of reference to the human part of risk management shows how narrowly we focus on current risk management as a practice. This is probably due to the fact that traditional risk management has been associated with health and safety in the workplace. Logic dictates that any accident must be as a result of some oversight, that if identified, can be corrected. The almost total neglect of the human factor, this narrow focus of risk management has managed to creep into every aspect of modern life, especially those areas where the negative consequences, however unintended, threaten to be greater than the benefits.

In Positive Risk Management, risk taking and risk aversion are viewed as complementary. You consider them to be of equal importance and value, within the appropriate context. It can also be seen as complementary to the traditional risk management paradigm. Introducing much needed balance, particularly with a focus on management skills and decision-making, it really brings risk management into perfect alignment.

You need to take a look at your organization, and at the roles that are better suited for those with an appetite to take risks, and the roles that are best suited to the risk averse. You can then place the right people in the right jobs, ensuring that your risk management efforts are not wasted. Granted, you will still need a solid risk management strategy, but with all the right pieces in the right places, this will be remarkably easier.

You will need to be able to identify the different appetites for risk in your organization or business. **_Positive Risk Management_** relies on the ability to identify these individual differences in the propensity for risk taking. You need to be able to assess personalities, an area of science that has seen much development over the last decade.

Because of the development of this science, the structure of personality assessment has seen much consensus. Human nature is becoming more and more understood also, and as a result, the positive aspects of risk management are all the more attractive to the development of your strategy.

The Five Factor Model of personality is a measure of personality that has shown relevance in many different cultures. It has shown that it remains consistent over much of your adult working life, as well as to be significantly heritable. This framework has many strands, which have a clear relationship between risk tolerance and risk taking.

Can Akdeniz

7. Risk Management And Business Continuity

Risk management is really the lifeblood of your business. It is a systematic approach, one that selects the most cost-effective ways to minimize the effects of risks on your business. You can never fully avoid risks in your enterprise. You cannot even completely mitigate all of the effects of these possible threats. Financial and practical limitations will always be present, regardless of the size of your organization. You need to, therefore, accept at least some level of risk, however residual.

Risk management could tend to be very pre-emptive, and as a result of this pre-emptive nature, business continuity planning was invented. The aim of BCP is to handle the results and consequences of residual risks, once these have been realized. Business Continuity Planning has become very necessary, especially since even the most unlikely events and risks will take place, given enough time.

You could view risk management and BCP as overlapping or rival practices, as is often the case. However, these practices are quite closely knit. Risk management results in the important inputs for business continuity planning, such as assets, or impact assessments, or even cost estimates. Risk management therefore covers areas that are vital for the business continuity planning process, as well as proposes some of the applicable controls for the risks observed. BCP goes beyond risk management though, in that it assumes that the risk will definitely occur at some point.

8. Risk Communication

This is complicated, to say the least, as far as cross-disciplinary fields go. Risk communicators have several problems, including reaching the intended audience, delivering the risk in a comprehensible manner, relating it to other risks, respecting the audience's values as these relate to the risk, and then predicting the audience's response. As a goal, risk communication strives to improve collective and individual decision-making, and is in a way related to *crisis communication*.

There are a few cardinal rules for *Risk Communication,* and its practice, and these include:

- Accepting that the public and other customers are legitimate partners
- Involving the public and other customer
- Planning and evaluating your efforts with a strong focus on your business and personal strengths, weaknesses, opportunities, and threats
- Listening to the stakeholders, noting their specific concerns

- Honesty, frankness, and openness are key
- Collaborate and coordinate with credible sources
- Meet the media needs fully
- Be clear, articulate, and speak with compassion

This is why *risk communication* is complicated, because it involves human beings. *Human nature* can therefore not be ignored in your *risk management strategy*! Regardless of the communication tools available to you, what is obvious is that, risk communication serves a purpose. In contrast, when you communicate threats and vulnerabilities, you will have a harder time managing them on your own, and you may not enjoy the support of your staff!

Conclusion

You may justify risk management by pointing out to how it protects value. This is true, but risk management can do a lot more to help your business excel. Risk management enables you to make better decisions, from corporate strategy, to major projects. Operational decision-making can benefit greatly from risk management. With timely, reliable and current information, you can make decisions of a higher quality!

Optimized and sustained performance is almost guaranteed, as a result of more risk-intelligent management. By anticipating possible risks, your business can become more agile. It will be able to respond quickly, whether to mitigate the impact of risk, or to maximize opportunity for gain.

Risk management can be described as a comfortable pair of shoes. You will not realize the value of these shoes until you have had them on your feet for a while. To see the value of risk management, you just need to ask a CEO if he would like to give up his effective risk management program.

Remember what happened to the businesses in the Great Depression who did not have risk management plans in place? I didn't think so, because nobody remembers those companies at all today!

About the author

Can Akdeniz is entrepreneur, consultant and book author. He is regarded as one of the most inspiring business authors of our time.

His books address an array of important business topics from general topics like productivity to more specific topics like the value of being seen as a "cool boss." In addition to running the acclaimed business blog businesshacker.co .

Can has released numerous books that have collectively changed the way people think about business and achieving success.

Check More Books by Can Akdeniz
http://www.amazon.com/Can-Akdeniz/e/B00DJPQA34/

Can's Blog
http://businesshacker.co

Follow on Twitter
https://twitter.com/canakdeniz1981

CPSIA information can be obtained at www.ICGtesting.com
Printed in the USA
LVOW08s0853130816

500246LV00006B/431/P